1

Andrew's Gift

Carl Hoegerl

Edited by

Nyla Wolfgang

Printed and distributed by Lulu Publications.

Table of Contents

Preface

Perhaps, once in a lifetime, you encounter a story like nothing you've ever heard before. A story that is so inspirational that the world must hear about it. This is one of those stories.

This is a story of a boy named Andrew. Andrew was full of life and he inspired all those who were around him. He was a giving person who continued to give to others even after his death. This book is dedicated to his life and to what his life meant.

This book is an attempt to tell his story. I am not a professional writer but I realized that this story needed to be told. This story needs to be told to the world far and wide. It's a story made up of stories that are hard to bind into one story. What I do know is that it starts with one person who unknowingly affects many. It is full of twists and turns. It shows the love of God in so many ways.

This is not a long book; it reads more like a short story. It is meant to be a short read that will inspire others to give of themselves, to help others, and to love God and one another.

I hope that you enjoy the book and encourage others to do the same.

Proceeds from this book will be used to help others who are less fortunate get the education they deserve.

Sincerely,

Carl Hoegerl

Chapter 1 – July 4, 2004

The family stood huddled together around the hospital bed grasping at what little hope remained. The body before them was lifeless and pale. A tube snaking out of the young man's mouth was attached to a machine that breathed for him. They had never seen anything like this before.

Only twelve hours ago they had all been preparing for an evening of picnicking and fireworks. But on this Fourth of July there would be no family picnic or fireworks for Andrew's mother, father, and four brothers. The six of them stood in total shock consumed by the magnitude of this tragedy. They looked expectantly at him for a sign that the body still held life. A brief finger twitch. The slight rise of his chest regardless of the machine. But there was nothing. Not one single movement.

As Andrew's father stood by his son's bedside, he could only think about his repeated attempt to keep Andrew from buying the new ATV. He knew that Andrew was independent and had a tendency to do things on his own, but he still felt responsible for Andrew's accident.

The entrance of Dr. Reich into Andrew's room jarred the family from their individual thoughts. Dr. Reich's face was expressionless; not even a glimmer of hope could be found in his eyes. He looked quietly at Andrew, and then briefly glanced at the family before dropping his gaze. His chin sunk to his chest as a tear rolled from the corner of his eye down his cheek. Closing his eyes Dr. Reich simply said, "I'm sorry."

Those two words knocked the collective breath from the family as they were hit with the realization that after just eighteen short years; Andrew's vibrant life was over. A mix of emotions overwhelmed the family. Their strong faith gave them strength because they believed Andrew would be leaving his battered body to go onto better things. They knew that Andrew's soul would be set free. At the same time they began to mourn the loss of their son and brother.

Through the fog of raging emotions Andrew's mother realized that Dr. Reich was speaking. He was saying that the head trauma was so severe that Andrew was technically brain dead. He would not be able to breathe on his own again without the aid of machines.

Dr. Reich had known this wonderful family for years. Their kids had grown up together. How could this be happening to them? This could be one of my own kids thought Dr. Reich as he gently wrapped his arms around Andrew's mother. Neither one of them could really grasp what was happening.

The family stood quietly around Andrew's bed holding hands to form a protective semi-circle around his still body;

11

each person lost in his own thoughts. After wiping tears from their eyes and taking a few calming breaths, the family walked out of the room knowing that they needed to update family and friends, who were waiting in the lounge, on Andrew's condition. The lounge was crowded with loved ones and the unspoken worry that their worst fears were going to be confirmed. As Andrew's father explained what Dr. Reich had told them, the room collapsed into a mess of tears, sobbing, and Kleenex. Friends clung to one another and family members did their best to offer consolation to Andrew's parents.

After what seemed like hours, they were interrupted by an unfamiliar face. The woman was dressed in plain clothes, wore glasses, and carried a small clipboard. She introduced herself as Louise and offered her condolences to Andrew's family. She spoke softly and reassuringly but with a bit of urgency to her voice. She knew that it was a difficult time for the family but she wanted to talk to them about organ donation. Louise explained that even though one life was being taken, many more could be saved through Andrew's sacrifice.

Chapter 2 – Ten months earlier

Beep-beep-beep-beep. Looking down at the pager that runs my life I see the dreaded numbers: 876. This code means I'm needed in the ER for another admission. Just as my eyes start to close again, the pager beeps urging me off the cot and into action. Stumbling toward the door of the lounge, I wonder, yet again, why do I do this? For the past week and a half I have been on call every other night. I'm not sure how many more twenty-four hour shifts I can handle. The lack of sleep and the stress is starting to take a toll on me, but there is nothing I can do about it now. Wearing my stained, but once pristine, white lab coat, I run downstairs to the E.R. as my stethoscope bounces against my chest.

Rounding the corner of the E.R., I run into Keith, the emergency room resident.

"Mr. Henderson is having chest pains again."

I feel the stress weigh my shoulders down at the news. "What room is he in?" I ask tiredly.

I grab Mr. Henderson's chart from the clerk's desk en route to his room. This is the fourth time he has been to the E.R. this week. Mr. Henderson is a paranoid schizophrenic with stomach ulcers. Even though he is only 34 years old, he is convinced he's going to die of a heart attack. Every time he comes to the E.R. I tell him that the bad food he eats upsets his stomach and that if he would eat healthier he wouldn't have to worry so much. Or bother me so often! I think walking into Room 10.

Mr. Henderson is holding a small plastic basin to his mouth where remnants of vomit speckle his lips. "Get away from me! I don't want to see you! You disgust me! You threw me out of the E.R. the other night!" Unfortunately, I feel pretty much the same about him. This is not going to be an easy night.

In my most reassuring doctor voice I tell Mr. Henderson, "You're not having chest pain Mr. Henderson. It's your stomach."

"Not this time. I haven't eaten anything all day and I keep up-chuckin even the water I drink."

"Maybe it's your medication," I say.

"Maybe you need medication Doc," Mr. Henderson says. "I have chest pain, belly pain and I can hardly breathe. It ain't the meds. I can't have any of them anyways cause nothins stayin' in my stomach."

"Let's take a look at you. Lie down, relax," I say, pulling off my stethoscope to listen to his heart and lungs.

"Everything sounds good Mr. Henderson. Let me have a nurse do an EKG on you and we'll take it from there."

17

I can't stand patients like Mr. Henderson. They come to the E.R. every other night at 2:30AM and waste your time. Patients like him take me away from those who really need my time and expertise. Again the broken record plays in my head, why do I do this?

Walking down the hall I stop the first nurse I see. "Hey Jill, will you do an EKG on Mr. Henderson in Room 10?"

"Not him again?" I know she's not any more thrilled than I am to have to deal with Mr. Henderson's chest pains again.

"Yes," I say. "This time he's got shortness of breath and vomiting too. I'll be back in 10 minutes. I'm going to get some coffee. Do you want some?"

"Sure," Jill says over her shoulder. "Milk and lots of sugar too, don't forget!"

The familiar doctor's lounge is decorated in old plaster that's been painted over and over again for the past thirty years. Two over-used sofas are the only places to relax but I'm pretty sure they are both original to the hospital. As I pour stale coffee from the pot, Dr. Seymour walks in the door. He's one of the hospital's attending physicians. In his late forties, Dr. Seymour has been practicing internal medicine for almost 20 years.

"Hey Dave," he says to me holding out a paper cup for me to fill with the mud the lounge tries to pass of as coffee.

"What are you doing in here at this hour? It's 3:00 in the morning," I ask.

"I got called in to see one of my patients who we ended up sending to the ICU. She's pretty sick," he replies.

"I thought the days when you were called in at 3AM were over once you become an attending?"

19

"Not so my friend," he says. "As for me though, they will be over soon. I'm gonna leave clinical practice. I've found a job in the biotechnology field with fixed hours, no call, and best of all, I don't have to listen to patients complain anymore. I'll be out of here in two weeks."

As he says this to me, my mind is thinking about the many articles I have seen recently about doctors, lawyers, and other professional people leaving their careers for something else because they are fed up with all the stress and they want something new.

"I've lost my passion for medicine, Dave," Dr. Seymour says to me. "I just can't do this anymore."

Here stands my worst fear right before my eyes. I'm not alone in my feelings about the medical field. I'm not sure if this is reassuring or unnerving. Before my thoughts can wander too far, the annoying "beep-beep-beep-beep" of my pager beckons me back to the E.R.

Over the loudspeakers comes the announcement "Code blue, E.R., Room 10."

Someone's heart has stopped working, and that someone is Mr. Henderson. Throwing my coffee in the sink I run down the corridor to Room 10. Mr. Henderson's face is blue and he's not breathing. Nurses and E.R. techs are running around everywhere. Feeling for a pulse I find nothing.

"Get a crash cart," I yell to one of the nurses as I kneel down to give Mr. Henderson two quick breaths before starting CPR.

"1 n 2 n 3 n 4 n ..." I say as each compression is given. The cycles repeat several times, first breaths given, then compressions one after the other.

While I give chest compressions, Jill frantically tries to put EKG leads on. "We need epi now," I shout. Keith draws up the epinephrine and with one quick squeeze, the epi flows into the IV. Jill is still intensely feeling for a pulse. I don't think she's ever going to find one when she says, "I've got a pulse!" Sighing with relief, I stop chest compressions as Mr. Henderson's face starts to lose the blue tinge. A cheer goes up from the staff gathered in Room 10 as Mr. Henderson's pulse strengthens and he breathes on his own.

"We've got a pulse but it's weak. He's not breathing well. We may need to intubate him and send him to the CCU."

I'm surprised to see Dr. Seymour walk into the room. "Are you still here?" I ask.

"Yeah, I figured I better stick around when you got called. I thought you might need some help. Let's intubate this guy" he says grabbing an intubation kit. On the first try, Dr. Seymour inserts a tube into Mr. Henderson's mouth and down his trachea. We continue bagging Mr. Henderson until we are able to hook up to mechanical ventilation.

Knowing that Mr. Henderson is out of the woods for now, everyone starts to calm down. The staff begins to take off their gloves in preparation for the mountain of paperwork that goes along with any code.

I finish my paperwork while continuing to see other patients throughout the night. In the morning I stop by the CCU to check on Mr. Henderson before finally going home. Mr. Henderson is awake but still intubated, so he cannot talk to me, but there is a smile on his face. I'm surprised to see him smiling at me after his agitated tirade from the night before.

"How are you doing?"

Mr. Henderson motions for me to hand him some paper. He writes out the question, "The nurses tell me that my heart stopped last night?"

"Yes."

Then he writes words I've needed to hear: "THANK YOU."

A weird feeling comes over my body as I stand there looking at Mr. Henderson. I realize for a moment that we have done something good. Even amongst all the chaos of a busy emergency room and endless paperwork, we had saved a man's life. With teamwork and perseverance, we had restarted a man's heart. For that moment, any thoughts or feelings of fatigue leave me and seem trivial. I simply respond by saying, "It's my job."

Mr. Henderson just smiles.

The weird feeling quickly vanishes when my pager beeps again. Freaking pager! I want to go home. This time it is the clinic where I moonlight. I forgot that I switched call with Jose. I won't be going home to sleep after all. My first patient has arrived signaling the start of another busy day.

Chapter 3

Arriving at the clinic 40 minutes late for my first appointment, I stumble into the door of the exam room. Sitting on the exam table is a tall 17 year old adolescent with brown hair and a smirking grin. .

"You must be Andrew."

"Yep, that's me," he replies, still smirking.

"What are you here for?" I ask.

"I'm here only because my mom told me to come. She worries about everything. I've had this persistent cough now for a week. I don't really feel the best. I seem to be coughing up this green stuff too," he says with a big smile.

"Let's take a look here. " I insert the tongue depressor into his mouth where white spots cover his tonsils and the back of his throat. "Here, let's take a culture" and before he has a chance to say "no," I gag him with a cotton swab.

"Dang it Doc, did you have to do that so quickly?" Andrew sputters. "That thing tastes like crap."

"Yeah yeah, I know. We're going to send it off for strep to see if you have strep throat. You've got white spots all over the back of your throat. I'm going to give you a prescription for some cough drops until the cultures come back. If the cultures are positive, we'll start you on antibiotics. If the cultures are negative, we'll keep you just on the cough drops."

"You mean to tell me you're not going to give me any antibiotics after I made this trip in here?" Andrew asks.

"Like it or not, that's the way it is," I reply.

"Fine, call me with the results." he says storming out of the room.

28

Moving through the rest of the day from one patient to the next, I notice that I'm becoming increasingly tired and irritable. Simple things that the patients do or say make me feel upset. I realize too that the patients are becoming more inpatient with me.

Walking down the hall, I stop to take a breath. I try to brush mounting concern from my mind figuring that I'm letting the patients get to me. However, in the back of my mind is the thought that I have been feeling this way ever since I came back from a mission's trip to Guatemala.

After 10 hours at the clinic, I arrive at home and crash on the couch. The sun shining through the curtains wakes me the next morning. Yet another day where a quick shower is my only moment of peace before returning to the chaos and confusion I left just a few hours earlier. It is another day just like the one before it and the one before that.

After you do a job like this day in and day out, you can't help but think how monotonous it is. You may ask yourself, how can a doctor say that? How can a doctor say that their job is boring? But if you think about it, all we do is listen to people complaining all day. Whenever someone has a problem, they come to us and we listen to them complain, then we give them a drug that may or may not work.

After punching the alarm again, I realize that the intensity of the sun shining in my eyes means I have overslept. I am late – again. Jumping up I rush to the bathroom where I brush my teeth, run a comb through my hair and throw on the same clothes I wore yesterday. Then it's out the door and back to another day of listening to patients' complain.

Worrying that I'm almost an hour late, I run into the clinic only to find that my first two patients have cancelled.

Although I'm slightly relieved, it is a huge frustration that patients do not seem to understand the value of my time.

I spend another day just seeing one patient after another, listening to patients complain about their snotty noses, their coughing spells, their diarrhea and constipation. Boy, it's really nice to finally leave the clinic and have a chance to let loose and party with some friends.

Chapter 4

Heading home after hanging out with some friends, I notice that my heart is racing. I have been feeling out of breath for most of the night, but chose to ignore it. The hospital is on my way home and I am breathing in short gasps by the time I reach the parking lot. I park right in front of the emergency room and walk through the automatic doors clutching my chest.

The first person I see is Keith. "What's wrong, Dave?" he asks, coming toward me.

"I'm so freakin' short of breath, I'm having palpitations" I struggle to respond.

"Have you ever had this happen before?

"No, not ever. I have been feeling this way recently and then tonight it suddenly got worse."

"Here, get in this wheelchair, let's get some oxygen on you and get a chest x-ray," he blurts as he wheels me down the hallway.

"Wait here," he says.

Sitting in the wheelchair outside the radiology department, I feel my airways clenching around my throat. It feels like there are a thousand bricks on top of my chest. I have never felt this way before. A little minor asthma in the past, but nothing like this helpless feeling. Nurses, residents, and others walk by and I feel like I can't even talk. Finally I catch my breath.

After 15 minutes of sitting alone in the hall, a woman comes out of x-ray and asks if I am Dave. "Yes," I reply.

"Well then, let's go get some x-rays," she says wheeling me through a double door.

After spending about five minutes moving in all different directions going from x-ray to x-ray, I am finally seated back in the wheelchair. I am wheeled into a noisy room with patients all around me. Only a thin curtain separates me from the next person. One of the patients on the other side of the room is a young boy yelling at the top of his lungs as they stitch up a laceration. The guy next to me is obviously drunk. I can smell the vodka evaporating from him as he sings at the top of his lungs.

There I was, on this side of the curtain. I was not used to being the patient. Usually I was the guy on the other side.

The nebulizer treatments that they gave me did help; after some time, my breathing is better. I look down at my feet and notice that they are very swollen. What is going on with me? I'm only 28 years old and I feel like I'm 98.

The curtain slides open and there is Keith. I haven't seen him in almost two hours since I first came into the E.R.

35

"Dave," he says, "your x-ray is showing some heart failure. Are you feeling OK?"

"I'm doing OK," I reply. "What's causing it?"

"That's what we don't know. Have you ever had problems like this in the past?"

"No, only had some minor asthma in the past, but nothing major."

"Any foreign travel recently?"

"Yeah, I was in Guatemala about two months ago on a mission trip helping to take care of some of the people there." I said.

"Maybe that's it," he said.

"What?" I said

"Sometimes when people go to foreign countries they pick up something and sometimes a virus can do something like this." he says.

"That's not good."

"Well, regardless of what caused this, you're going to have to be admitted. I'll start taking care of the paperwork now. Do you feel alright at this point?"

"I feel fine. Much better than I did before, that's for sure." I reply.

I have no idea what just happened to me. What was going on? I'm supposed to be the doctor, not the patient.

As I lie there thinking, I feel myself falling asleep. Maybe this is just a dream. I try pinching myself to wake up, but the pinch hurts. This is real.

Chapter 5

Waking up the next morning, I quickly realize that this is not a dream. I, the doctor, am lying in a hospital bed still in the E.R. Even though I am still short of breath, I feel a lot better than the night before.

While I am using the urinal, the curtain is abruptly shoved aside. All five members of the cardiology team stand before me.

"Greetings," Dr. Brown says.

I frantically try zipping up my pants, but succeed only in dropping the urinal on the floor.

"Don't you guys know how to knock?"

"Sorry," Dr. Brown mutters.

That's all the more apology I get as Dr. Brown continues. "Since you are all set, let's get started. I heard the team say you came into the hospital last night and had some trouble breathing. Your chest x-ray shows some heart failure. We don't know why. Sometimes this can be related to a virus, but many times the cause is unknown. We're going to do some tests today to see what's going on here. We know that it's not your asthma but it could be your heart. "

"What kinds of tests are you going to do?" I ask.

"We're going to start with a heart ultrasound and possibly a cardiac catheterization. Any questions?" Dr. Brown says.

"No, I guess not." I say.

And with that, all of the members of the team leave. Here I am in this hospital all alone. My family is two hours away. I haven't told them what's going on. I know that if I tell my mother she will worry too much. She is not supposed to worry about me anyways. I'm the doctor. I'm not supposed to get sick. Doctors are supposed to be immune from patients.

Despite feeling better, I still feel short of breath. The medication has helped but it seems like it's not working the way it should be. A man with a wheelchair interrupts my thoughts.

"Time for your echocardiogram" he says.

I get into the wheelchair and away we go. Throughout the day I am subjected to one test after another. The pace is rather grueling and I continue feeling short of breath. I almost think I am getting worse. Near the end of the day I undergo a cardiac catheterization. A catheter is inserted into an artery in my groin and fished up to my heart. Then dye is injected into me so that the doctors can look at the valves and arteries around my heart.

I wait in the recovery room for Dr. Brown. When he returns the news is not great.

"The normal ejection fraction is about 50 to 70%. Yours is only 5%. Although you are responding to some of the medications, I'm afraid we're going to have to send you to a larger medical center where they have the specialists to handle your situation. We're going to send you to Philadelphia first thing tomorrow morning."

I can't believe what I am hearing. This isn't happening to me. I'm a DOCTOR. I'm not supposed to get sick.

Just then a nurse comes over to my bed. She is very polite and says, "I'm Colleen. Is there anything I can get you?"

"No," I say.

"If there is anything I can get you, please let me know. I'm going to take you to your room," she says.

We have a nice conversation on the trip up to my room. She asks about my family. Then she proceeds to tell me about her family. Colleen has five children at home – all of them boys. Her face glows as she tells me about each of her sons.

Not only does Colleen have a real love for her family, but she seems to like her job as well. She greets each person we pass in the hallways on the way up to my room. As we reach the door to my room, she asks if I have any children. I say no. "Well, if you ever have that chance, they bring joy and a sense of purpose to your life," she says. Colleen helps me into my bed then tells me that if I need anything to just let her know since she is my nurse for the evening.

Alone in my room I finally call my mother to tell her what is happening. She is in complete disbelief at what I am telling her. She says she is on her way and drives through the night just to be with me the next morning.

It has been an exhausting day and I feel tired. Colleen peeks into my room to make sure everything is comfortable. I watch her work and realize that I have seen her around the hospital before. I never thought she, or any other nurse, would be taking care of me one day. My eyes began to close and I finally fall asleep.

Chapter 6

"What's going on?" I ask myself. I am abruptly awoken from sleep. I am on a gurney being rushed down the hallway. Things seem confused and all that I feel is a swishing feeling rushing across my face. There are people all around me hanging IV bags, checking my heart, checking my lungs and asking me questions.

I realize very quickly that I am no longer in my hospital bed. Instead I am on a helicopter being rushed to Philadelphia because my heart is failing worse than before. When the helicopter lands, I am rushed to ultrasound. My ejection fraction has fallen to less than 2%. It's hard to believe that I can survive with an ejection fraction that low. Most patients would have died.

When they discover that my ejection fraction is so low, they immediately take me to the operating room. During a

6 hour operation a mechanical device, called a bi-ventricular pump, is implanted into my chest. This machine will become my heart for the next eight months.

This mechanical device works almost like an artificial heart. Using my heart and this machine, blood can be pumped throughout my body. It doesn't work as well as my original heart, but it is the only thing keeping me alive. Without this machine I'd be dead.

This machine is not without its complications. It doesn't pump very well and it's easy to get blood clots which can lead to other complications, including a stroke. As a matter of fact, during this whole ordeal I do suffer a stroke. It is severe enough to knock out a significant portion of the right side of my brain.

When I wake up I am in a foreign place – a hospital room hooked up to machines. I am on a mechanical ventilator, intubated so that I could not breathe on my own, and have IVs all over my arms. My memory is not that good. I cannot move my left side. No matter how hard I try, I cannot get my left arm to move.

Here I am, a physician, trying to help others. I go on a mission trip to Guatemala, come back, have heart problems, and almost die. Then I suffer a stroke. What could be worse?

I see a nurse off in the distance. Of course I cannot yell to her because I have a tube in my throat. Then, very quietly, I hear someone whispering in my ear. I turn only to see a doctor. He is a short man with a beaming smile.

"I'm Dr. Gomez. You're just starting to wake up. Do you know where you are?" he asks.

"That's ok. It's hard to talk with that tube in your throat. You have suffered a stroke. It's going to affect the left side of your body. Anyway, I'm going to be your doctor here. I am a cardiac surgeon. Your heart is in really bad shape. We had to put a bi-vat machine in last night. It's going to help your heart pump blood throughout your body. This also means that you are being placed on a cardiac transplant list. We're going to have to find you a new heart. I spoke to your parents last night. They know what is going on. In fact, I think your mom is just right outside. I will go get her." Then he disappears.

I can't believe what's going on. I need a new heart? How can this be? What did I do to ever deserve this? Why can't I just keep the heart that I already have?

Out of the corner of my eye I can see my mom coming. She is moving rather fast and has a very scared look on her face. She comes over and gives me a big hug. I try to move but notice that I can barely move my right arm. Nothing else is moving. Then I remember I have had a stroke. Nothing on my left side can move. I can't talk. I can't move. What good is having a new heart?

As my mom gives me a hug, I feel something cool run down my cheeks. It is one of my mother's tears. *"I'm tough, I can handle this"* I think to myself. With those thoughts, I began to weep. For the next 10 minutes I cry like I've never cried before. My mother just holds me in her arms.

The ventilator keeps making sounds and alarms keep going off. Every time I cry it interferes with the settings on the ventilator. Soon, I cried myself to sleep. I knew that my parents were there, which gave me comfort.

The next two days I spend in the intensive care unit. After two days, they take me off the ventilator and I am allowed to leave the ICU. I have my own hospital room. I can finally talk. But I continue to have a large machine that I have to carry everywhere that I go. It is like being chained to a bowling ball. No matter where you go, it goes

too. But I also know that this machine is helping me to

live. It is my lifeline.

Chapter 7

My hospital room had a window overlooking the streets of Philadelphia. You can see the Philadelphia skyline in the distance. Looking down on the streets below me can see people rushing and hustling about their daily routine. Every one of those people down there can walk and talk without any problems. How many times did I take for granted the simple ability to walk? Now I cannot even take a simple step without falling.

Dr. Gomez and his team come in morning after morning to see how I am doing. They always say the same thing, "Any day now you will get a new heart." This cycle continues for days that turn into weeks that turn into months. After a while it is difficult to keep my hopes up; I begin to wonder if I will ever get a heart.

One day I stopped Dr. Gomez and said to him, "Don't get picky, any heart will do."

"No, no," he says. "It has to be a good heart. I'm not going to just settle for any old heart."

I am also consumed by the idea that someone else has to die in order for me to get a new heart. The only thing I have to rely on is my faith. God has a reason for everything. He always has a plan, even when we don't understand why something happens. Our minds are incapable of understanding what this plan is. I pray every night that if God's plan involves taking someone else's life, then could I have the gift of life and a new heart.

After eight months of prayer, physical therapy, and up and downs, anyone can lose hope. I see the hope in my parents' eyes starting to diminish. My father often paces the hallways. My mother leaves the room for an hour or two at a time. I realize that it is their way of coping with things. It isn't easy for me, but in some ways, it is worse for them.

I cannot be confined to my room for so many hours at a time. So, the medical staff devises a way that I can carry my bivat machine around with me. They put it on wheels, so that I can carry it around like an oxygen tank. I start roaming the halls because I am able to walk better. I still have a limp when I walk but I'm able to walk on my own. There are many other patients down the hall from me that I have not met before. By being able to walk around on my own with this tank, I am able to start visiting with my neighbors.

I meet Ryan who is two doors down from my room. He is around the same age as myself and is engaged to be married. He ended up getting a viral myocarditis, just like me. He has been here for over 10 months is still waiting on a new heart. Over the coming months, Ryan and I become

53

good friends. He is a teacher at a local high school and was engaged to be married two months prior to coming into the hospital. When he got sick they decided to postpone the wedding.

Then there is Olivia, who is 52 years old. She suffered a massive heart attack. Olivia's been waiting for a new heart for two months now and is also on a bivat machine. Some of the nurses say that she may not make it much longer. They say that her heart is too weak to last.

The hospital's great because they try to plan events for us. Once a week they have a band come in and play for us. It's a young band who likes to play a lot of Christian rock music, which I enjoy listening to. Once in a while we might get a visit from a local reporter who wants to do a news article about us. Last month, Ryan got a visit from a local TV station. They ran a story about what happens when you get on a heart transplant list. They showed him

54

with his bivat machine and waiting to get a heart. They showed what a typical day was like just being here in the hospital room day to day.

I'm just too young for this. I was once a busy resident physician and then in a matter of hours my life changed dramatically. Sometimes I feel that I reached my final days too soon. Is this what it's like being in a nursing home? Sometimes I just walk down the hallway looking out the windows. Sometimes friends visit. Sometimes family visits. My mother's here all the time. I would just like to go home.

As I lay down to go to sleep that night, I hear a lot of hustle and bustle outside my room. Nurses are running around. Looking outside my room, I catch a glimpse of Dr. Gomez. "What's going on?" I yell to him

"Ryan's getting a new heart," he replies.

"That's great" I say. I try to be very happy for Ryan but inside I can't help asking myself, *What about me? Where is my heart?*

A few minutes later I see a bed being whisked down the hallway. As Ryan's face flashes past my room, he hollers, "I'm getting' a new heart. Pray for me Dave."

I take a few minutes and ask God to be with my friend and get him through this trying time. My friend deserves a new heart because he has a full life still ahead of him. He is engaged, wants to have children, and wants to live life to the fullest.

The transplant team works tirelessly all night and into the early morning hours.

The next morning when I wake up, one of the nurses comes in to give me breakfast. I notice that there is a tear in her eye. "How is Ryan?" I ask afraid of the answer.

56

She proceeds to tell me that Ryan did not survive the surgery. What is left of my heart sinks about two inches deeper into my chest. Tears begin to roll down my cheek because I cannot believe what I have just heard.

Not only have I lost a friend but I can't help thinking to myself, what if that were me? Sometimes I feel selfish with some of the thoughts that I have – I just don't want to die.

During the next week, I find out that Olivia died too. That means that out of all the patients in the entire wing waiting for an organ transplant – only two of us are waiting for a new heart.

Chapter 8

"Dave, Dave, wake up." It is 4 o'clock in the morning a few days after Ryan died and a nurse is trying to wake me.

"Dave, we just got word that we found a match. You're going to get a new heart."

Mom is so happy when I call to wake her up with the news. "I'm going to get a heart."

I have to hold the telephone away from my ears because the only thing I can hear on the other end is a loud squeal of excitement. I've never heard her so excited.

"Dad and I are on our way," she yells.

While my parents make the four hour drive to Philadelphia, nurses are rushing around my room getting things ready. One nurse checks my equipment, while another is trying to clean everything in preparation for surgery. I've never seen anything like this before.

Dr. Gomez comes in to see me. "Now it's your turn Dave," he says putting a stethoscope on my chest. "You're in tip top shape, ready for this one," he comments.

"Dr. Gomez'" the nurse says as she takes the thermometer out of my mouth. "His temp is 101.5 degrees," she whispers.

I knew what that meant. That means that I won't get my heart. If there are any signs of an infection, that puts your name further down on the transplant list and it becomes someone else's turn to get a heart.

Dr. Gomez can see the disappointed look on my face.

"I'm sorry my friend, not this time" he says quietly.

Chapter 9

"Aren't they beautiful?" comments Mom.

"Yes they are," I answer.

The only good thing about my hospital room is that I have a great view of the fireworks downtown. It is the Fourth of July and, unfortunately, I am still stuck in the hospital. No celebrations for me this year – just another day in the hospital.

"It's getting late Dave, I think I'm going to go over to the hotel room and call it a night," Mom comments.

"Ok Mom, don't worry about me, I'll see you in the morning."

My parents usually either stay at a local hotel or with my cousin who doesn't live far out of town.

As my mother left that night, I saw out of the corner of my eye a tear roll down her cheek. She really has gone through a lot. She comes down every week and spends at least 2-3 days with me. The rest of the week she works at home to maintain her job. They live about four hours from here.

My cousin and mother leave the room only to go downstairs and sit down on a bench outside the main entrance. They are talking and crying about the whole situation. It is a brisk July night. A cool breeze comes through the parking lot in front of the hospital.

"I know everything happens for a reason, but it's been eight months now of just waiting. How much longer is God going to make us wait?" my mother asks.

Just then, a low voice came from the background saying, "It won't be long now. He'll have a new heart very soon." A man is sitting on a bench across from my mother and

62

cousin. He is a tall, thin, African American man. He takes a puff of his cigarette and blows out slowly, "You girls have lost your faith. God will give you the gift when the time is right."   My mother looks over at my cousin and says, "He's right. When God decides, that will be the time."

"What's your name?" she asks the man.

"Bruce," he says breathing out another cloud of smoke. "God knows who you are and how much you've been praying. He listens."

"It's just hard after a while and you begin to lose hope. We've been waiting a long time for this," she says.

"I know, but have faith, the time is soon" he insists.

Mom turns to my cousin for a moment and smiles. When she turns back, Bruce is gone.

My mother yells, "Hey, Bruce?" into the parking lot hoping to find him, but there is no sign that a man was just sitting across from them.

I think an angel came to visit my mom that night.

Chapter 10

I fall asleep quickly that night. Since it was a holiday, there were a lot of visitors. My parents came to town for the celebration and we watched fireworks from my room.

Every night as I lay down to sleep, I always pray that I will get a new heart. I fell asleep quickly after my prayer tonight.

At about four in the morning, I am awakened. Once again nurses rush around my room.

"It's your turn this time, Dave" one of the nurses says.

"Where have I heard that before?" I reply.

"Oh, come on Dave," she says kindly. "I've taken your temperature; there is no sign of a fever this time. I think you're going to get it this time."

I lean over and dial my parent's cell phone. I hear the tired answer on the other end and say, "Mom, I think I'm getting a new heart. This one's mine. There won't be any problems this time."

I can hear the hesitation in her voice. She is hesitantly excited. "This is it, I can feel it," I say to her. "The angels have told me that this one is for me."

Just at that moment, Dr Gomez walks in. He greets me with a smile like he always does. "Dr. Hollobaugh," he says, "today looks like a good day for you to get a new heart."

"But what is it going to be this time" I ask.

"Nothing, this is your heart," he replies. "This heart is a young heart. This is the perfect heart for you Dave."

I can't help thinking about the disappointments that I've had before. I don't want to get my hopes up when

66

everything might just fall apart in front of me. Even as I start to get more excited, I know that there is another family out there suffering from the loss of their loved one. It's a very unusual feeling – almost a guilty feeling. I want to live, but I know someone else has died to make my wish come true.

The nurses are getting me ready to go to the operating room. In the pre-op area, I can't help but notice another patient beside me. She seems a little nervous.

I lean over and ask, "What's your name?"

She hesitates for a moment and then says, "Barbara."

"Are you here to get a new heart too?" I smile.

"No," she says, "I'm getting new kidneys."

"Well today is our day. I'll see you bright and cheerful after the surgery," I say as we are both wheeled off to different parts of the pre-op area.

67

Then I catch a glimpse of my parents. They see me and quickly came over to give me a big hug.

It is a long time after that of just waiting. The transplant team had to go halfway across the state to get my new heart. While my mother uses the restroom, my father says, "You know Dave, this may not work out. This organ may not be the right one for you." I can see the concern on his face. "He told us so. I know this is my heart, he told me so," I reply.

"Who told you so?" he asked.

"God told me this morning. He came and said, 'David, my son, your donor is here with me in Heaven and your heart is on its way.'"

At that moment, they wheel me into the O.R. to get my new heart.

Chapter 11

In the O.R., the anesthesiologist asks me my name and birthdate. She says, "We're going to give you a new heart today." She slips the mask over my face and the lights go out quickly. From my perspective, the operation goes by really quickly. After being put out, I remember being in a long narrow tunnel holding someone's hand. He looks rather young, maybe around twenty years old. He says to me very plainly, "Don't worry; you're going to make it through this just fine. I'll be with you the entire way."

I remember his words to me and then looking down this long tunnel and seeing a bright light near the end. I ask him what this light is and he says, "That's where I live now. That will be your home one day, but not yet. It's not your time yet."

With those words, I wake up. Dr.Gomez is smacking my face saying in some very quiet words, "Wake up Dave, you now have a new heart."

I immediately wake up. I have a smile on my face. Although I am still on a respirator, I know that will be taken off very soon. I notice that I am no longer hooked up to the bivat machine and I won't have to haul it around anymore with me wherever I go.

As they bring me to the recovery room, I look over at the patient next to me. I notice that it is Barbara, the other transplant patient I had met before going into surgery. I raise my hand and say, "Welcome to the other side" as best I can with the bipap mask still on me. She smiles.

She looks tired and says in a very quiet voice, "You too and guess what, no more dialysis."

I give her a thumbs up and quickly roll over to rest for a while.

Not long after that, both my parents are there. I tell my father "See, I told you this one was for me." He just laughs.

Chapter 12

It's been nearly a month since my surgery. I feel great. My heart is working well and there have been no major problems. I have to have biopsies of my heart every few weeks to make sure there are no signs of rejection. I have to take 17 different pills every day for various reasons. Some of the medications are to keep my blood thin; some are to keep my body from rejecting the heart.

Today I received a letter from the donor family. It read as follows:

August 24, 2004

Dear Recipients,

We received a brief synopsis on who received our son's organs. We were glad to hear that everyone is doing well.

We wanted to share some information about our son Andrew.

First of all, our son Andrew made the decision to be an organ donor when he renewed his driver's license. This was his wish.

Andrew was our middle child. He had two older brothers, Ryan, 23 and Steven, 21. He also had two younger brothers, Daryl, 18 and Daniel, 16. Sorry, no girls.

Andrew was a typical boy, loved to fish, hunt, water ski and ride his ATV. He just graduated from high school and planned on working with a special friend learning the field of excavation. He worked last summer and throughout the school year on weekends riding and playing with heavy equipment. This wonderful friend had employed Andrew at his ice cream shop originally. Andrew did not like the sanitation aspects of the food industry, in other words, he didn't like to clean up. They offered him a job in their excavating business instead. In return, they brought such happiness to Andrew and our family. He was truly happy.

Another thing that made Andrew smile was his niece, Rhianon, 10 months, and nephew Weston, 5 years old. He loved them. As any uncle does, he would wind them up and pray they would settle down when they went home.

Andrew was a clown; he loved to make people laugh and smile. We will always remember that smile on his face. He was always there to help anyone in need. He had a sensitive heart for others.

We hope that we can share with you many wonderful memories. We look forward to hearing from you and hope that you are all doing well.

Sincerely,

Dan and Colleen

*****

I put the letter down as tears hover in the corners of my eyes. I can't help feeling a little guilty. I feel guilty that I am alive, and Andrew is not. I tell my feelings to my parents, but even after an extensive conversation the only sense I can make out of this is that God has a plan and part of that plan is that I would have Andrew's heart.

It takes me several weeks to muster up enough courage to write back to Andrew's parents. My hands tremble with sadness and happiness as I write:

Dear Colleen and Dan,

My name is David. I am a 32 year old male heart transplant recipient. I wish you never had to read such a letter as this and those of the others that your brave loving Andrew gave the gift of a second chance too. I can only hope that my words can offer you all some peace at such a difficult time in all of your lives. Thank you so much for honoring Andrew's wish to be an organ donor. Thank you so much for raising such a compassionate and amazing young man as Andrew. Thank you for sharing your memories of the remarkable young man that saved my life!!

I want you to know that I prayed for Andrew the whole time I was waiting and the day that I was told a heart was on its way. I told my parents I knew that because God told me that morning he had my donor in heaven with him and everything was going to be o.k. This was important to me because more than I wanted to live I wanted Andrew to have eternal happiness! Based on what I have been told about Andrew, I have no doubt that he will. I promise I will not take one day for granted and I will honor Andrew's memory as much as I possibly can.

We have all been blessed because such a wonderful young man as Andrew walked on this earth. I am sorry that you lost him at such a young age but take comfort in knowing that he loved and was surely loved more than some people who are here for a hundred years. God bless you all and help you through this difficult time.

My prayers are with you.

Signed, David

*****

Over the next several months, Andrew's family and I send letters back and forth. I would send one and then a of couple weeks later, I would get one in return. Their letters made me look forward to getting the mail.

As the months pass, I regain my strength. The days are long and filled with occupational and physical therapy. My heart is strong and working very well. For the first year, I have to get biopsies of my heart every month. That basically requires a cardiac catheterization to be performed every month. A catheterization means that a catheter is inserted into my groin and advanced to my heart. Once in my heart doctors take a biopsy of the muscle tissue and send it off for testing. This gives the doctors an indication if my body is trying to reject the heart. I also have to take mountains of medications every day in order to prevent my body from rejecting the heart. If the biopsy shows signs of rejection, my medications may need to be changed or altered. Worst case scenario? I would need another new heart transplant, but so far everything has worked out well.

*****

I have been corresponding with Andrew's family for a year now, but we still have not met in person. I am very anxious to see who they are.

Late one afternoon, after coming home from physical therapy, there is a letter sitting on the table. The return address is Danville, PA where Andrew was from. Opening the letter, I read the following message:

79

September 7, 2005

Dear Recipients and Families,

It has been 14 months since everyone received his or her second gift of life. Hopefully all is going well.

We have heard from some recipients and families and would like to continue with this communication. As I said before, our family looks forward to any correspondence we receive. It actually helps us to remain positive knowing that we have been able to help so many.

If at all possible, we would like to meet with all of Andrew's recipients and hear their story. We'd like to share our story as well. There have been many moments over the past 14 months when we wonder why all this has happened. Then we are enlightened by the reasons that God has chosen this path for us. All of Andrew recipients

80

are the largest reasons for this path. We hope that all of you are enjoying this gift and sharing with others the value of life.

The Gift of Life program requires that we must receive permission for contact with any and all recipients. Our family would like to be contacted by anyone who would like to meet with us. I believe that this is an important step in our healing process both for the donor family and the recipient family. We look forward to this future step.

Sincerely,

Dan, Colleen, and the Boys

*****

My eyes are filled with tears just like after reading their letter. This family has endured so much and has experienced so much tragedy, but they still want to meet me, and I so badly want to meet them. My mother sends an

81

e-mail back to Dan, Colleen, and the boys. It read as follows:

Dear Colleen,

We've received your information on October 29, 2005. I tried to call you on Saturday and just got the answering machine. I tried a couple of times and then decided that maybe God wants me to start our contact with an e-mail. I have written for a while but that does not mean I have forgotten about you and your family. I think of you all everyday as I've told you before. I light a candle every time I go to Mass for Andrew. I know it's a small thing compared to the gift that Andrew gave to my son. I just want you to know that your generosity is appreciated each and every day. I know that by now you know that my son is a resident in pediatrics. He said from the beginning of his illness that he felt that his new heart would come from the Danville area.

82

I hope that someday soon we can meet in person and be able to share the whole story of Andrew and David's life. It is a wonderful thing to know that there are still people in this world who feel the same as we do about life. David is an organ donor as well as the rest of his family.

Our daughter Danielle said that she didn't used to think that if something happened to her child that she could donate his organs. After this experience with her brother and being on the receiving end, she said she definitely would. I want to tell you once again how sorry I am that you lost Andrew. I cannot imagine how hard that has been for all of you. Please know that we're looking forward to hearing all about Andrew when you're ready.

Sincerely,

Patricia Hollobaugh

Chapter 13

Several more months pass before the big day arrives. After a two hour drive from Saint Mary's, PA to Danville, I am full of emotion as I am about to meet Andrew's family, the Marion's. The plan was for my parents and I to go to Saint Joseph's Church for Mass and then to meet the Marion's afterward. It was a special Mass dedicated to Andrews's life and the wonderful stories that have developed because of Andrews's story. It's clear to me that Andrew was sent by God. Not only did he touch so many people while alive here on earth, but he continues to touch so many lives after his death in so many ways. People can see, live, breath and have a better quality of life because Andrew lived.

The church is big and red and sits close to the street. As I approach, I realize that I attended this church many times as an intern. Now, here I am returning three years later to meet the family whose son gave me his heart. Mounting the steps, I take a moment to look around. The town hasn't changed much. It is still a very quiet town, especially on Sunday morning. The bells are ringing this morning with an extra sense of excitement. The sound gives me a sense of a new beginning that I have never experienced before. A sense of peace settles over me. I am no longer nervous about meeting the Marion family. A picture of Andrew flashes before my eyes.

Birds are chirping in the trees and blossoming flowers fill the air with a sweet spring smell.

We are one of the first to arrive at the church and quickly take our seats near the front. The church fills with parishioners and the special Mass begins.   Father Wheary starts the Mass by quoting 1 John verses 7 and 9, "'Beloved, let us love one another, because love is of

God… God sent His only son into the world so that we might have life through Him.'"

He then continues, "In this Easter season we are reminded of the new life gained for us by the death and resurrection of our Lord and Savior Jesus Christ. We are reminded that we are then to be life for one another, upholding one another, affirming one another… Loving one another, even to the point of death. And a dramatic example of this is the life of an 18 year old parishioner who designated on his driver's license that upon his death his organs were to be donated to others.

"Andrew Marion died in a 2004 ATV accident. Doctors at the Hospital moved quickly in accordance with his wishes and the wishes of his parents. Andrew was able to gift others with his kidneys, his heart, and his lungs.

"In a letter to all of Andrews's organ transplant recipients, his parents Dan and Colleen Marion, said that their son was a 'typical boy, who loved to fish, hunt, water ski, and ride his ATV… Andrew was a clown; he loved to make people laugh. We will always remember that smile on his face. He was always there to help anyone in need. He had a sensitive heart.'"

Father Wheary paused and looked out at the pews filled to capacity. He glanced briefly at his notes and took a breath. "Now I would like to tell you about the people who received Andrew's organs. Their testimonies come from a series of letters written by the recipients themselves to Andrew's parents and are used with their permission. These testimonies, I believe, underscore Jesus Christ's commands that we love one another and that through love resurrections to new life happen all the time.

"Andrew's heart recipient is a 31 year old medical resident, now living in Saint Mary's, Pennsylvania. His father wrote Andrew's parents that while in his son's hospital room right before the transplant surgery he said to his son that things might not work out, that the organ might not be the right one for him. David's father said that David told him God had visited him that morning and told him that this was *his* heart. David, himself, wrote Andrew's parents and confirmed his father's story. David told the Marion's that, 'I want you to know that I prayed for Andrew the whole time I was waiting and the day that I was told a heart was on its way I told my parents I knew because God told me so. He also told me that Andrew was with him in heaven and everything was going to be OK. This was important to me because more than I want to live, I want Andrew to have eternal happiness.'

"The lung recipient is a 65 year old father of two and grandfather of six and a military retiree. He wrote, 'Thank you for such a thoughtful, caring son. I'm really doing well since surgery.'

"And then just this month, I was the priest on a engaged encounter weekend in Colombia, Pennsylvania. I was sitting in a parlor to hear confessions when a young woman came in and began telling me about herself. She said, "'I used to have terrible kidney problems but I received a kidney transplant from an 18 year old boy and I am doing so much better.'" At the time I thought, 'This couldn't be?' I asked her a few questions and, lo and behold, yes, she is one of Andrew's recipients. When I told her that Andrew was one of my parishioners she couldn't believe it and neither could I. I told her that I performed his funeral two years ago and that I was preparing a homily on the entire story. Well, as you can imagine, she was astounded. And so was I, and we still are."

I was amazed to hear how God brought Barbara to Andrew's pastor – the pastor whom I had listened to three years early as an intern.

Father Wheary concluded by saying, "The most important thing is that we all have God's spirit within us. That spirit gives empowers us to love one another as Jesus loves us. 'This is my commandment that you love one another,' Jesus said. That could include designating organ donation on your driver's license. April is organ donation month. Do you want to be an organ donor?

"We can show each other our love for one another by something simple. It can mean a kind word, a smile, reconciliation with someone, a volunteer for a charity, or a donation. Let us help one another rise from the dead, in whatever way God leads us. Jesus said, 'It was not you that chose me, but I chose you and appointed you to go and bear fruit that will remain... This that I command you.'"

When Father Wheary finished speaking, the church was completely silent. No one made a sound. It was so quiet that I could hear the wind whispering in the trees outside. At the conclusion of his homily, the church was just quiet.

Father Wheary broke the silence by saying, "David and Barbara are here today. David and Barbara, please stand and let us see you."

As we stood, the church erupted into an applause so loud the whole town could hear. I stood there looking into a familiar face in front of me. Tears filled Barbara's eyes. My eyes then fell on another familiar face. A woman sitting with her husband rose and came toward me. Tears also filled her eyes. She was the nurse I knew from the hospital where I waited for my heart. She had helped to take care of me when I first went into the hospital. As she approached and gave me a big hug, she said, "I'm Colleen, Andrew's mother."

I suddenly realized that the mother of my donor was the nurse who helped take care of me while I was in the hospital. She was the nurse who was so proud of her family of boys and told me all about them as she wheeled me to my hospital room.

We just sobbed and hugged each other for what seemed like hours. Neither one of us could believe what was happening. The kind nurse who took care of me while I was in the hospital was the one who made the decision to allow her son's heart to be given to me. I just stood there thinking what a wonderful family I had just inherited. I am a living testament to their generosity. What this family has endured no one would wish on their worst enemy.

When the service ended, the Marion's, Barbara, my parents and I, spent the next several hours at a local diner going over stories and stories about one another. They told me about Andrew and I told them about what life was like being on a waiting list for a heart transplant. I learned that Andrew was a loving brother who always had a grin on his face. He would often get into trouble with his nieces and nephews, but he always found a way to laugh about it. I also learned that I had met Andrew before he died. The teenager whose mother had sent him to the clinic for a sore throat was Andrew. I stared in disbelief as Colleen told me this news. I could not believe that I had met the boy whose heart now beats in my chest.

Andrew left behind four brothers and two loving parents. I've never met a family quite like this one before. They all seem very close and one of the most loving families I've ever encountered.

Since that day, I have become the best of friends with Barbara and the Marion family. It's truly amazing how things go around in a circle sometimes. God is like a wreath, no beginning, no end, and if we do good unto

others, good will descend upon us as in a circle.

Chapter 14 – Barbara's Story

Even though this book is mainly about Andrew and David, Barbara's story is no less amazing and it deserves to be told. The following is the story Barbara told Father Wheary in the parlor during the engaged encounter weekend.

In 1988, Barbara was diagnosed with chronic interstitial nephritis. This is basically severe, malfunctioning kidneys. By 1994, she was on hemodialysis three times per week, three and a half's hours each day at Saint Joseph Medical Center in Reading, Pennsylvania. Hemodialysis uses an artificial kidney machine to cleanse the blood. The process is like working an eight hour day with cramps and headaches. Barbara could barely eat but was still trying to hold down a part-time teaching job. In 1995, she was placed on peritoneal dialysis. Barbara spent 11 hours each night hooked to a special machine to cleanse her blood. The procedure was gentler than the hemodialysis, but her condition continued to deteriorate. She was losing her sight, had no night vision, and was in danger of breaking her bones easily.

In 1996, she received a kidney transplant, but it had to be taken out the next day because her body rejected the organ. That same year Barbara lost both her husband and her brother.

In 2004, while at workshop, Barbara got a call that she was at the top of the list for another transplant. "God," she prayed, "please let me finish this workshop." The workshop ended on Friday and on Sunday she went to Lehigh Valley Hospital to get her new kidney.

When Barbara woke up she could tell that the operation was successful. She said she felt so rejuvenated. She also said she could smell better, taste better and just felt more like herself.

Barbara is now engaged to be married. She is completely free of all dialysis and she spends a lot of time outdoors hiking in the woods and working on a bat project with a local scientist. She carries around heavy stuff, which is something she couldn't do before.

Barbara says that she thinks about Andrew all the time. She even tries to make her teaching fun since he was a fun loving boy. Once upon returning from an excursion, she opened a letter from Andrew's aunt who said, 'If, after receiving Andrew's kidney, you find that you have a special love for the outdoors and for nature, you will know that it is Andrew's spirit with you.'

Chapter 15 – July 4, 2004 - Around the Campfire

Everything just felt like it was a blur. No one could believe what had just happened. We left the hospital with a huge void. How could this happen on the fourth of July? How could we lose our son, our brother, our grandson, all in one day?

The family, friends, brothers, parents, came home to Andrews house that night. Someone started a campfire and gathered chairs around it. We all sat around and reminisced about the life of Andrew.

He was such a kidder. We talked about the time Andrew caught the lawn mower on fire and then laughed about it.

How could you get mad at a smile like that? After catching the lawnmower on fire he had a big smile on his face.

He was always concerned about others. He once spent days fixing up the old ATV for his nephew. His nephew still rides the ATV to this day.

At that point, Andrew's mother said "do you remember Andrews graduation?"

Everyone nodded and shaked their heads.

Andrew's mother said , "at the end of the day on his graduation day he had so many presents and gifts that everyone had brought. There was a huge pile. I said to

102

him 'Andrew, look at the big pile of presents everyone has brought you.' But Andrew did not care. He had tears in his eyes because so many people had come to his party. He made the remark to me 'why did so many people come here just for me?' Andrew didn't care about the gifts that he received or the money he had received. It made him more happy just to know that so many people had come to his party. That was just the person he was. He didn't care about the material things of the world. He cared about touching others lives in ways that others couldn't. He always had a smile on his face."

Everyone sat in chairs and on the ground in a circle around the campfire. As his mother was speaking, everyone sat starring at the fire. Some were crying and some had tears in their eyes.

Andrew had touched his family in ways many only hope
to. He had left a mark on each and every one of those
people. He made them realize that there's more to life than
material things.

His mother went on to say, "tonight is only the beginning
of what Andrew will accomplish. We made a difficult
decision today. Andrew will continue to live on in the
hearts, bodies, minds, and souls of everyone he touched
both literally and spiritually. Andrew did not like to
receive gifts. He so loved to give to others and make
others happy."

At that point, Andrew's mother then spoke up and said
"let's pray the Lord's prayer." Together, one by one,
Everyone stood up and started praying the Lord's prayer.
As they wiped tears from their eyes and the first words
"Our Father" began to be said, a void could be sensed

being lifted from each and every one of them. It was as though Andrews spirit was coming into them and beyond.

Everyone knew at that moment that they had not lost Andrew. Instead, Andrew had given them a spiritual gift.

It is so fitting that Andrew be remembered as giving to others. Andrew lived a life of making others laugh, giving of himself, and living life to its fullest. The gifts Andrew has given us will continue to live on. His life, his personality, this story will touch the hearts and souls of generations to come.

LaVergne, TN USA
22 March 2011
221131LV00001B/35/P